BRIAN JOHNSTON

The Journey of the Ark

HAYES
PRESS Christian Publisher

Contents

1

Something Resembling Christ

Travelling is part of my lifestyle. On a deeper level, the Bible refers to Christians as pilgrims as we journey through life heading for heaven. Even in gentle strolls, it's good to have a travelling companion, but it's even better to think of how in our spiritual walk we're meant to know companionship with Christ. In Luke chapter 24, we read of how the newly risen Jesus came and went with two of his still dejected followers as they walked away from Jerusalem on that weekend when Jesus had died and risen again. What a difference their travelling companion made to their conversation that day! The apostle Paul commanded early Christians in Galatia to "walk by the Spirit" (5:25). The full sense of these words is "keep in step with the Spirit," which emphasises walking step in step with Christ each day. Just like the hymn says: "He walks with me and talks with me along life's narrow way."

In the days of Moses, God lived in a Tent known as the Tabernacle in the middle of all his people's tents. But the Tabernacle was a portable structure and often on the move as the people walked between encampments. The Tabernacle as God's house on earth then was God's resting place among his people, but it's especially touching to read in the Bible that when his people walked, God walked with them. One verse puts it like this: God "walked in a tent and in a tabernacle" (2 Samuel 7:6 KJV).

Whenever the Israelites broke camp, they transported every-thing associated with God's house, and, in particular, the sacred chest, or box, known as the ark of the covenant, normally located in the holy innermost part of God's house. This ark symbolized the Lord's presence among his people. As they moved from camp to camp, he travelled with them on their journeys.

I hope together we can learn lessons for today - for our daily walk with the Lord - as we recall some of the adventures of the ark as it travelled with God's people in those days. That's what we'd like to do by God's help: not considering the ark in relation to the rest of the furniture of God's Tabernacle-house, but only thinking of the ark. We'll aim to follow it - to go with it - on its travels, on its historical journey from Sinai to Zion, or Jerusalem, a journey which spanned something like 500 years.

It's at Sinai that we begin. That's Mount Sinai where the Israelites received the Ten Commandments from God. The ark was made in Sinai by a man called Bezalel. God equipped him with all the skill and wisdom needed to make it to God's own specification. Made of incorruptible wood covered with gold on the inside and outside, it contained the stone tablets of the Ten Commandments. In all three of these ways, in the incorruptible wood, the overlaying gold, and the fact that it contained the Law, we can view the ark as a very clear picture of Christ. The wood brings before us Christ's human nature in as much as it was incorruptible. But while God the Son became Man, he was always more than man - he never ceased to be fully God.

This clear teaching of the New Testament was prefigured here in the gold which overlaid, or covered, the incorruptible wood of the ark, both inside and out. And this gold-covered wooden chest kept the stone tablets on which the Ten Commandments were written which further illustrates the point we're making; for it was the Lord Jesus Christ alone who kept God's Law perfectly during all his earthly life here - even as Psalm 40:8 could be seen as prophesying he would when it said: "Your law is within My heart." So what a striking picture of Christ the sacred ark of the covenant became. Complete with its lid of pure gold which had a representation of angels over it, it became the place of communion between God and his people - or at least between God and the people's representative. But how did the ark come into existence? How was it made? This is what Exodus 35:30-33 says:

> "Moses said to the children of Israel, 'See, the LORD has called by name Bezalel the son of Uri, the son of Hur, of the tribe of Judah; and He has filled him with the Spirit of God, in wisdom and understanding, in knowledge and all manner of workmanship, to design artistic works, to work in gold and silver and bronze, in cutting jewels for setting, in carving wood, and to work in all manner of artistic workmanship.'"

The name of the man who was used in its construction, Bezalel, means "in the shadow of God." I believe he was a man who lived

3

up to his name, for why else was he chosen for such an honour as this: to be the craftsman of the ark which was a symbolic representation of Christ? We see that being in the shadow of God led to the formation of something resembling Christ. That's very instructive for us because Psalm 91:1 says, "He who dwells in the secret place of the Most High shall abide under the shadow of the Almighty." But how are we to dwell in the secret place? What did the Lord teach us in Matthew 6:6? He said: "When you pray, go into your room, and when you have shut the door, pray to your Father who is in the secret place." We get into the secret place when we pray alone to God. And with that we can link prayerful meditation on the Bible which 2 Corinthians 3:18 describes as a mirror, the mirror of the Word: "But we all … beholding as in a mirror the glory of the Lord, are being transformed into the same image from glory to glory, just as by the Spirit of the Lord."

And where will it all lead to? If, in the secret place of daily prayer and Bible reading we come close to God, even beneath his shadow as it were - what will be the end result? I'm sure there's a hint in Galatians 4:19 where Paul says, "until Christ is formed in you." It's just as we pictured it with Bezalel and the ark: being habitually in the presence of God, under the shadow of the Almighty, will bring about the formation of something resembling Christ. Not a sacred chest like the ark, but a life and character, our life and character, transformed to be like his!

This is something very precious and practical - a glorious possibility in our lives as believers. When we talk about Christlikeness we're not talking about something that's skin deep, not merely a superficial modification of our behaviour patterns to conform to the standard and expectations of a Christian subculture - but something far deeper; an inward, radical character change by one glorious degree after another. As we think of the Lord's earthly life: his self-sacrificing service, his love and humility, his non-retaliation and forgiveness and his faith and obedience, surely we really want to be more like him. It's been said that God's greatest purpose in us is to make us more human by making us more like Christ (see Romans 8:29).

We've seen how God used a man called Bezalel whom he filled with his Spirit, and equipped him for the task of forming the ark which symbolises Christ. From this, we've drawn the lesson that in every Spirit-filled life, lived out in the shadow of God, there will be the formation of a resemblance to Christ.

2

Christ-centred Obedience

We've seen from God's Word how the journey of the ark of the covenant was a journey which began at Mount Sinai. It began there for it was there that it came into existence at God's instruction. God used a man called Bezalel whom he filled with his Spirit, equipping him for the task of forming the ark which symbolises Christ. We previously drew the lesson that in every Spirit-filled life, lived out in the shadow of God, there will be the formation of a resemblance to Christ.

Now we want to illustrate the teaching, from the story of the ark on the move, of how God wants our lives to be Christ-centred lives. We come now to the book of Numbers, the fourth book of Moses. The book of Exodus deals with the Israelites being brought out of Egypt and coming to Mount Sinai, where on condition of their obedience, they become the people of God. God gives details of how they're to serve him and how he'll live in his Tent, or Tabernacle, in the middle of all their tents. Chief among the furnishings of that Tabernacle house in which God lived among his people, was, of course, the ark of the covenant or, as it was sometimes also called, the ark of the testimony.

The book of Numbers, which follows Exodus, is primarily taken up with what follows when the Israelites, now the people of God, journeyed on from Mount Sinai through the desert. Chapters 2 and 10 tell us that whenever they broke up camp to follow God's leading in the pillar of cloud by day and of fire by night they couldn't go forward in any old order. No, God said that the tribe of Judah along with Issachar and Zebulun had to set out first. Then came the tabernacle followed by the tribe of Reuben along with Simeon and Gad. Then came the ark carried by the Kohathites. The other Levites accompanied the tabernacle attending to its transportation. Following the ark came the tribe of Ephraim along with Mannasseh and Benjamin. Finally, bringing up the rearward was the tribe of Dan, along with Asher and Naphtali.

So, if we had been able to get a bird's eye view of the children of Israel as they moved across the desert sands we'd have seen the standards of Judah and Reuben going on before the ark and the standards of Ephraim and Dan coming up behind. In other words, the ark was central to the people on their travels. From that, I believe God wants to teach us that our life is to be a walk with Christ, the Christ who was symbolised in the ark long ago. More than that, he must be central to our lives as we journey on with God. It's a powerful reminder to me that God's Word is living and active, as Hebrews 4:12 says. For out of a chapter full of apparently dry instructions to Israel about the order of their march, there comes to my heart a challenge as to whether my life is a Christ-centred life or not.

7

As if to ensure the point wouldn't be lost on us, God made the ark very distinctive while on the move. Its uppermost covering was a blue cloth. Everything else connected with God's house was transported under leather coverings. So the central, blue-covered ark would be particularly striking. All the more so, because God had made a particular association with the colour blue. In the fifteenth chapter of Numbers we find the story of a man who broke God's Law by going out and gathering sticks on the seventh day, the day of rest. After consulting the Lord, Moses was told to put the man to death for his disobedience. To prevent such a thing being repeated, God commanded there and then that all Israelites should attach a cord of blue to the bottom of their robes - the idea being that whenever they saw one another's robes they'd be instantly reminded of the need to obey God's commands. In other words, God associated the colour blue with obedience.

Remember that while on the move through the desert, the ark was visibly covered with a blue cloth. Later in history, God was able to look down on the perfectly obedient life of his Son, Jesus Christ, as He journeyed around among the Israelites of his day, in particular as surrounded by the twelve apostles. Listen to how the apostle Peter gives a little thumb-nail sketch of that wonderful life, the most beautiful this world has ever known. These words are taken from his preaching to a non-Jewish audience as recorded in the book of Acts chapter 10:36-40. Actually, in the view words that follow, it's almost as if we have a summary of the whole of Mark's Gospel.

> "The word which God sent to the children of Israel,
> preaching peace through Jesus Christ - He is Lord

8

of all – that word you know, which was proclaimed throughout all Judea, and began from Galilee after the baptism which John preached: how God anointed Jesus of Nazareth with the Holy Spirit and with power, who went about doing good and healing all who were oppressed by the devil, for God was with Him. And we are witnesses of all things which He did both in the land of the Jews and in Jerusalem, whom they killed by hanging on a tree. Him God raised up on the third day, and showed Him openly."

The hymn says:

'We will remember His wonderful life,
Doing Thy will.
Perfect obedience midst sorrow and strife
Led Him to Calvary's hill.
Jesus our Lord
Loving and giving each step of the way.'
(Psalms, Hymns and Spiritual Songs 81)

How true! What a wonderful life of obedience to his Father's will. That the point the apostle Paul emphasises in the famous bible passage found in Philippians chapter 2:7-8: "… but made Himself of no reputation, taking the form of a bondservant, and coming in the likeness of men. And being found in appearance as a man, He humbled Himself and became obedient to the point of death, even the death of the cross." There it is, there's the obedience – so totally characteristic of that life of the Lord Jesus here on earth. Surely, his God and Father had looked forward to it from the days of the Old Testament shadows; remember the Bible tells us the Law and all associated with it were simply shadows projected in advance of the reality that was coming in Christ. The ark draped all in blue cloth, processing in the midst of the people as they traversed the desert sands is just one of those delightful shadows we get of the striking obedience of Christ as he went about doing good in the centre of the twelve apostles and all the surrounding crowds.

And what of us today? Is our obedience noticeable? In the measure that Christ is truly central to our lives it will be! Paul speaks of others glorifying God for the obedient confession that some Christians were giving to the gospel of Christ (2 Corinthians 9:13). May God help us to live lives that are Christ-centred, in which our obedience is as strikingly different as the blue-covered ark was from all the other tabernacle furniture when on the move.

3

Handling with Care

I f you've ever been camping, especially part of a group camp, you'll know something of the effort that's involved in breaking up camp and moving on or going home. It's so much easier, of course, when there are many expert helpers who know exactly what to do and they simply get on with it. Just imagine then the job of taking down the Tent known as the Tabernacle in Moses' day and preparing all its structure, and furniture, for transportation. Surely it was good that the three divisions of the Levites knew their individual duties well.

Those of the family of Gershon had responsibility for transporting the coverings and curtains and courtyard hangings. To assist them they had two wagons and four oxen at their disposal, according to Numbers chapter 7. Then we read in chapter 4 of that same book that the family of Merari had the even heavier task of conveying the boards and pillars with their heavy sockets and bars. Just as well they had four wagons and eight oxen at their disposal, twice as many. In contrast, the remaining third branch of the Levites, the Kohathites, were not given any wagons or oxen. Their special responsibility was for the ark of the covenant and the other holy furniture of the sanctuary. And concerning it all, Numbers 7:9 says, "they carried [them] on their shoulders." In particular, they bore the ark on their shoulders whenever they moved camp. To do this, chapter four tells us they used staves that were part of the original design of these furniture items, so that they didn't so much as touch any of the objects themselves, especially the holy ark of the testimony.

As we remember that this sacred chest of the ark of the testimony specifically symbolized the Lord Jesus Christ and that God's servants then weren't to touch it, nor to transport it on carts, but rather to bear it on their shoulders, feeling its weight, perhaps we're reminded of the need today for care in our handling of the testimony of Christ - how careful we need to be as we bear witness to him in the gospel. Nothing in our presentation - nothing in our lifting up of the Saviour - must jar with the gospel of the glory of Christ.

The apostle Paul and his co-workers in gospel mission work provide us with a good example. There was nothing casual about their approach as we can see from their report in first Thessalonians chapter two, the early verses:

> "But as we have been approved by God to be entrusted with the gospel, even so we speak, not as pleasing men, but God who tests our hearts. For neither at any time did we use flattering words, as you know, nor a cloak for covetousness - God is witness. Nor did we seek glory from men, either from you or from others, when we might have made demands as apostles of Christ.

But we were gentle among you, just as a nursing mother cherishes her own children. So, affectionately longing for you, we were well pleased to impart to you not only the gospel of God, but also our own lives, because you had become dear to us. For you remember, brethren, our labor and toil; for laboring night and day, that we might not be a burden to any of you, we preached to you the gospel of God. You are witnesses, and God also, how devoutly and justly and blamelessly we behaved ourselves among you who believe as you know how we exhorted, and comforted, and charged every one of you, as a father does his own children."

There, in his letter to Thessalonian converts, Paul speaks about how God had entrusted him with the gospel - just as a householder entrusts his property to his steward. But more than that, Paul saw himself as being like a nursing mother and, at the same time, like an encouraging father to the new converts at Thessalonica - those to whom he had preached the gospel of God (v.9). In preaching, he'd acted like a herald making a public proclamation. So he was conscious, wasn't he, of the heavy responsibility he bore in the matter. He and his co-workers saw themselves as stewards, mothers, fathers and heralds in all their communication to, and concern for, those who were coming to faith in Christ.

They spoke not as pleasing men, but as pleasing God who proved their hearts. There's a great danger today, as always, in the preacher seeking to court popularity by setting out to please his audience at the expense of God's truth and at the expense of faithfulness to Christ. The preacher may be tempted to pander to current fads or endeavour to make his message socially acceptable by minimising the offence of the cross. Paul was not a preacher like that – since his aim was to please God, not his hearers. Let's learn the lesson from the handling rules governing the picture of Christ we get in the ark of the testimony: that we're most definitely not to tamper with the Gospel of Christ. Its content is untouchable, but some today, as in Paul's day, are preaching a different gospel (see Galatians 1).

From a reading of the first chapter of Paul's first letter to the Church of God at Thessalonica, we can see something of the calibre of these converts – what a testimony and influence they bore, extending to far beyond their own neighbourhood. They had become the talk of the region. Surely this was in no small degree due to the purity, clarity and quality of the preaching of the preachers we've been hearing about in chapter two. Paul speaks there of being affectionately desirous of those Thessalonian converts; of imparting not only the gospel but his own soul also; of working day and night; of behaving faultlessly and of giving fatherly encouragement. No wonder the message had such an impact in the first century! Can we match up to such a love for souls? Is our lifestyle so transparently sincere and open and accommodating? Are we as selflessly diligent? With as high standards for ourselves – practising what we preach?

We mentioned in the last chapter that the ark was covered over while on the move between camps. This in itself was not unique, for the same was true of the other articles according to Numbers chapter four. But the case of the ark of the testimony was quite unique in terms of the number of its coverings and the order of them. First, it was covered with the beautiful veil that separated off the holiest compartment within the Tent of Meeting or Tabernacle. When everything was being dismantled in order to move camp, the priests covered the ark with that veil that hung between the two rooms - even the privileged Kohathites who would bear the ark were never to see it uncovered in the sanctuary. Then over the ark went a second protective covering of leathery material corresponding to the outer Tabernacle covering. Finally, there was the outermost, visible covering of the blue cloth with its association with obedience - as we already saw from Numbers chapter 15.

In terms of those coverings, let's recap: there was the attractive veil, the way to God, speaking beautifully of Christ, then there was the protective leather, and then the blue cloth. May I suggest that in adorning the preaching of Christ today, as we bear testimony, there are three things we must ensure are covered:

- that first and foremost in our testifying we present not ourselves but the attractive Christ of God - present him clearly as being the only Way to God that there is. No-one can come to the Father except through him (John 14:6);
- second, that we protect our witness from any damaging trends which endanger the purity of the Gospel of Christ;
- and finally, that from our own obedient lives we, like Paul, challenge our hearers to obey the Gospel. The blue colour denoting obedience reminds us again of the example of Paul who never shrank back from declaring the whole counsel of God. No 'easy believism' this, but a costly discipleship - one that's true to all the New Testament Scriptures.

4

A-B-S-E-N-C-E Spells Defeat

F irst moves are usually important. Ask anyone who plays chess or listen to anyone who follows the fortunes of Formula 1: those first moves between grid and first corner often determine the race pattern. In Numbers chapter 10, we read about the first move of the ark of the covenant away from Mount Sinai. Remember it was at Mount Sinai that it had come into existence. It had been built there according to God's design by a man by the name of Bezalel. In this book, it's as though we're travelling with the ark, that's the ark of God, or ark of the covenant, back in the days of Moses. What we want to try to do is to draw contemporary lessons from principles written long ago for our learning. At last we're getting underway on this long 500-year journey with the ark from Mount Sinai to Mount Zion and its resting place in Solomon's Temple.

We've made mention that, from the information given to us in the Bible book of Numbers, we discover that generally, as a rule, the ark went in the middle of the people of Israel as they went from one camp to another through the desert. In that way, we've already emphasized how Christ, whom the ark represents, ought to have the central place in our pilgrim lives today. But first moves, as we've said, are indeed significant, and the first move of the ark after nearly a year at Sinai was quite exceptional because it didn't go forward in the centre of the Israelites as it usually did, but went on ahead of them.

We're entitled to ask ourselves the reason for this departure from what was the norm. Perhaps, the reason was connected with Moses' request to Hobab, when he asked him if he'd lead them on their journey. Moses was asking Hobab to be their guide because of his great experience of the desert. It's immediately after that, that we read about the ark going out in front instead of in the middle. It was possibly a lesson to Moses concerning his lack of faith. Not Hobab, but God would lead the way, and Moses must trust him.

The apostle Paul in his letter to the Colossians chapter 2:6 tells us that we're to walk in faith today. Just as we received the Lord by faith, it says, so we are to walk by faith in Him. Then there's the principle found in Matthew's Gospel chapter 9:29, as the Lord speaks with the blind beggars and says: "According to your faith be it done to you." If you're like me, then your response to such words as these will be "Lord, increase our faith." God is the God of the increase, and he'll surely increase our faith if we seek that blessing from him. We long, day to day, to know, and to be able to trust fully, his leading in our lives - just as emphatically as when the ark most unusually went on ahead and the people followed it.

Four chapters later in the book of Numbers - a book largely

taken up with the failures of God's Old Testament people in the desert – we come to the point when, after sending the spies in to spy out the promised land of Canaan, the people showed a distinct lack of faith by rebelling at the good testimony of Joshua and Caleb. They refused to go in and possess the land that God was promising would be theirs: they'd been swayed by the bad report of the other 10 spies – a report about the giants and all the dangers of the land.

But, as if this wasn't bad enough, once they heard of God's displeasure at their lack of faith and rebellion, they immediately presumed to go up into the land in spite of orders to the contrary. But the Bible makes the point very clearly that the ark of God remained in the camp. In other words, in contrast to earlier when the Lord had been leading his people by going ahead of them, as demonstrated by the ark taking the lead, now the Lord was most certainly not with the company of the people who belatedly attempted to reverse their earlier rebellion. And then, as always, absence spells defeat.

Without him, the Lord assures us in John 15:5, we can do nothing. If only Israel had realised that true safety lies in experiencing the presence of the Lord, not merely in knowing the absence of danger. To steer clear of the giants wasn't the safe course of action in the days of Moses, because the Lord wasn't with them. On the other hand, there was no danger for the disciples in Jesus' time when they were with him in the middle of the storm on the lake of Galilee – at least there was safety in the danger because the Lord was present with them in the situation. Once again, safety isn't the absence of danger, it is the presence of the Lord.

I'll never forget a Northern Irish Christian woman quoting that to me when living with her young family in the middle of "the Troubles." As we looked out through the window, soldiers were carrying out exercises outside – within a short distance of the house. It was then she said to me: "Safety is not the absence of danger, it's the presence of the Lord." Perhaps, you too, today need to hear that in your circumstances. It's certainly one clear lesson we can draw from Israel's experience with the ark in Numbers 14 – its absence spelt danger and defeat for them then. Moses, of course, was someone who knew how absolutely essential the practice of the Lord's presence was. His communion with the Lord immediately after the incident with the golden calves ran something like this:

The Lord tells Moses "I will not go up in your midst." Moses replies: "You say that I enjoy Your favours. If that's so, teach us Your way so that You'll not leave us. There's no point to us proceeding to Canaan without You." Then he gets to the heart of it when he says: "If Your presence doesn't go with us, don't bring us up from here. For what will be the difference between us and the other nations then? How will anyone know that we enjoy Your favours?" Then God answers his servant and says: "I'll do this thing you ask" – in other words "I will go up in their midst after all."

It always staggers me to think of how God was prepared to forego his desire and postpone his plan to reside among his people! Because of their serious failure in turning aside in the matter of worshipping the golden calves, God had intended to remain outside their camp, holding private communion with Moses at a distant tent of meeting. But Moses, true leader that he was, again interceded with God. He boldly asked if the privilege that was his could be extended to all the people. What about us? Romans chapter 5:2 tells us that Jesus has procured for us a permanent, though unmerited, audience with God the Father. Do we value that? Do we ensure we have a daily meeting with God, a time when we practice his presence?

There's another striking thing we find in Luke's Gospel chapter 2:44. There, we're told of the time when, as a boy, Jesus stayed behind at Jerusalem. His parents travelled for a whole day towards home "supposing Him to be in the company." I find it striking that, after going for a whole day's journey, it finally dawned on them that he really wasn't somewhere in the crowd of pilgrims, and they had to go back looking for him. What I want to say to us is this – let's not even travel through one day of our life's journey without having asked the Lord to go with us. Let's be sure to take the supposition out of our travelling each day by making sure we consciously practise his presence. In doing this, we'll be positively like Moses, and not like the people who presumed to go forward without the Lord's presence among them.

One reason it's so important to know the Lord with us – is a reason we've seen illustrated just now with the ark of the covenant, and it's just this – that his absence spells defeat for us.

5

Looking to Jesus

We've already seen how the ark got underway, and how its first move was a break with the procedure set out in advance for its travels. The fact that the ark initially went ahead, rather than in the centre of the people, impressed on us again the need for faith, and for following God's leading in our lives.

Over the next forty years of desert journey, the Israelites would have broken camp and moved on something like once a year, though some of their stays were long and some were short. It says: "at the commandment of the Lord they journeyed and at the commandment of the Lord they encamped." And every time, following the usual practice, the ark would have travelled in the centre of the procession and been carried by its staves on the shoulders of those Levites who belonged to the family of Kohath.

When Joshua eventually took over from Moses as the leader of the people, and the people stood on the brink of entering - at last - into the promised land of Canaan, we come to our next adventure with the ark. At the Jordan river which stood between Israel and the land that was theirs by promise, something extraordinary again takes place involving the ark. Forty years before at the Red Sea, when the waters divided to let the people cross, it had come about by Moses stretching out the rod of God which symbolised God's power - power that was demonstrated in rolling back the Sea. Now at the Jordan it's the ark, called "the ark of His strength," that symbolises God's power over the waters. In another break with convention, the ark once more precedes the people as it's carried by the priests into the river first of all.

Now that's another thing - the Bible says it was carried by the priests at this point, not the Levites. Since the priests were themselves descended from the appropriate family within the tribe of Levi this may not be something different, but just a different way of saying it. Either way, it must surely have something to teach us. In fact, this is one of only 4 times in the Bible record of the movements of the ark when it's said to be carried by "priests" as opposed to "Levites" - and that record covers 500 years. The other times are at Ebal, at Jericho and when entering Solomon's Temple. We'll come to those in due course, but let's focus on the crossing of the Jordan.

In Joshua chapter 3, the ark is mentioned no less than 10 times. Obviously, the ark, as representing the Lord's presence, was crucial to them entering the promised land of blessing. When the feet of the priests who were carrying the ark stood in the shallows at the edge of the swollen river, the way opened up for Joshua and the people to cross on dry land. The ark then was stationed in the middle of the riverbed until all the people were safely across. Now what's the lesson?

Usually it's suggested that the river Jordan is a picture of death, but I don't believe that's ordinary, physical death here. Canaan, on the other side, the land of promised blessing, surely represents our inheritance. But the teaching is for now. This drama in Israel's history corresponds to our entering into the full enjoyment of every spiritual blessing in the heavenly places - and that's to be our present experience as chapters such as the first of Ephesians shows. There we read:

> "Blessed be the God and Father of our Lord Jesus Christ, who has blessed us with every spiritual blessing in the heavenly places in Christ, just as He chose us in Him before the foundation of the world, that we should be holy and without blame before Him in love, having predestined us to adoption as sons by Jesus Christ to Himself, according to the good pleasure of His will, to the praise of the glory of His grace, by which He has made us accepted in the Beloved.
>
> In Him we have redemption through His blood, the forgiveness of sins, according to the riches of His grace which He made to abound toward us in all wisdom and prudence, having made known to us the mystery of His will, according to His good pleasure which He purposed in Himself, that in the dispensation of the fullness of the times He might gather together in one all things in Christ, both which are in heaven and which are on earth - in Him" (Ephesians 1:3-10).

23

What a wealth of spiritual blessing is contained in these opening verses alone! We're meant to live in the enjoyment of them now, but, like Jordan in a time of flood, sometimes there seem to be impossible barriers between us and such victorious Christian living. We find it hard to claim the promises and realize the blessings. It's hard to set our mind on the things that are above (Colossians 3:1,2). The crossing of the Jordan reminds us that something needs to die first, before we can fully enter into the possession of God's promises in our life and service for him. We need to die to self.

But how does that take place, you ask? Well, in Joshua 3 verse 3 the people were instructed about looking at the ark. It was just as though Joshua was pointing out to the people "behold the ark" (cp. v.11) even as John the Baptist would later point out Jesus and say "Behold the Lamb of God" at that same Jordan river. The ark, of course, is a picture of the Lord Jesus and the power of God in Christ. We can do what's impossible in our own strength as we look to him and live in the power of his resurrection. Like Peter when he stepped out of the boat on the sea of Galilee to go to Jesus – he was all right so long as his eyes were fixed on the Lord, but when he looked at the waves instead he began to sink. It's like that with us.

With him all things are possible (Matthew 17:20). Pictured at Jordan in the ark of his strength, it is he who divides the waters or, in our case, the barriers that come between us and victorious Christian living. Christ's power is greater than all that would separate, or keep us back, from the blessing God intends for us. Knowing and practising the presence of a powerful Christ brings us into blessing and a real experience of spiritual realities.

That's why the practising of his presence is so important. And, in the ongoing challenges of life, many Christians have been comforted by the promise made by God, though made originally to Israel, "when you pass through the waters I will be with you" (Isaiah 43:2). At all times, and especially in times of difficulty, we need to maintain a clear view of him - just as every Israelite's eyes must have been on the ark as they passed through the Jordan into the promised blessing.

With this the writer to the Hebrews agrees, when in chapter 12:2-3 he writes: "... looking unto Jesus, the author and finisher of our faith, who for the joy that was set before Him endured the cross, despising the shame, and has sat down at the right hand of the throne of God. For consider Him who endured such hostility from sinners against Himself, lest you become weary and discouraged in your souls."

6

Death and Resurrection

As we follow the ark on its journey, now with Joshua, I want us to stay a little longer by the River Jordan. In the last chapter we saw how the ark had been instrumental in crossing over the river and entering into the promised land. God wanted his people never to forget that experience. To serve as a reminder to them, he instructed them through Joshua to set up a monument of stones. In fact it may well have been two monuments or two piles of stones – read the passage carefully for yourself. It's from Joshua 4:

> "And the children of Israel ... took up 12 stones from the midst of the Jordan, as the LORD had spoken to Joshua, according to the number of the tribes of the children of Israel, and carried them over with them to the place where they lodged, and laid them down there. Then Joshua set up 12 stones in the midst of the Jordan, in the place where the feet of the priests who bore the ark of the covenant stood ... and those 12 stones which they took out of the Jordan, Joshua set up in Gilgal ...

saying: 'When your children ask their fathers in time to come, saying "What are these stones?" then you shall let your children know, saying, "Israel crossed over this Jordan on dry land for the LORD your God dried up the waters of the Jordan before you until you had crossed over ..."'

From that reading it seems that there were two piles of stones - one set up on the riverbed while it was dry, and the other set up on the far side, in the promised land, made from stones taken from the riverbed. Those stones on the riverbed would, of course, soon be hidden as the water of the river Jordan returned to its accustomed flow and covered over them. There's a significance, surely, in the fact that there were hidden stones and there were public stones. Isn't that the way of it in much of our Christian experience: without the inner, hidden reality there'll be no evident, outward power in public. Take prayer, for example. Our standing in public at the prayer meeting will only be as effective as our kneeling in private in the secret place with God, hidden away from view.

But I think these hidden and public stones - one set under the water and one set on the riverbank - have something deeper to teach us. One set of stones was put into the river and submerged, the other was brought out of the river. Doesn't that remind us of the teaching of Romans chapter 6? Romans 6:3-11 says:

"Or do you not know that as many of us as were baptized into Christ Jesus were baptized into His death? Therefore we were buried with Him through baptism into death, that just as Christ was raised from

27

the dead by the glory of the Father, even so we also should walk in newness of life. For if we have been united together in the likeness of His death, certainly we also shall be in the likeness of His resurrection, knowing this, that our old man was crucified with Him, that the body of sin might be done away with, that we should no longer be slaves of sin. For he who has died has been freed from sin. Now if we died with Christ, we believe that we shall also live with Him, knowing that Christ, having been raised from the dead, dies no more. Death no longer has dominion over Him. For the death that He died, He died to sin once for all; but the life that He lives, He lives to God. Likewise you also, reckon yourselves to be dead indeed to sin, but alive to God in Christ Jesus our Lord."

The message of those verses in Romans chapter 6 is telling us of our need to realize and remember that we're to see ourselves as having died with Christ to sin - think of the stones put into the river - and also that we've been spiritually raised with him from the dead to live for God - think of the stones taken out of the river. In our case the reminder isn't stones but disciple's baptism in water. By the action of going into and coming out of the water we declare that we see ourselves as identified with Christ in his death and resurrection. Unless we recognize these two realities - that we've died to sin and that we're now alive to God - we'll not fully be able to live in victory overcoming the power of sin in our lives as believers.

In our consideration of the Jordan crossing we were thinking especially of our need to see the Lord and His power with us in order to live the life, claiming God's great and precious promises. As the ark had been with the people in the middle of the river, so we encouraged one another to discover the Lord Jesus with us as we go through difficulty and overcome obstacles by his power and presence. It's the idea of seeing ourselves with him - with him in his death and resurrection experience. We're not working towards victory, but from it - the victory Christ won for us at the cross. Sin, in our lives, hasn't been destroyed but it has been dethroned. In Romans chapter 6 Paul argues that we don't have to go on sinning as though we're powerless to overcome by the Lord's help.

In that chapter Paul says a lot about "servants" or perhaps we should say "bondslaves" to emphasize that what's being described is the type of service that absolutely bound a person to his master. Usually only death brought release for the bondslave. Throughout his life of service, which was often since birth, he had no opportunity to do his own will - but his will was totally swallowed up in his master's. That's exactly the imagery that Paul applies to us in this sixth chapter of Romans. Prior to conversion, we were "bondservants of sin" (v.20). Sin had dominion over us in our unsaved days. But now listen to the wonderful news that at the time of our salvation "we died to sin" (v.2). As with the slave in Roman times, it's this death - a spiritual experience in our case - that releases us from lives dominated by sin. Sin was our master, but no longer, for death - death to sin, has released us. Sin "shall not have dominion" over us (v.14).

As the hymnwriter says about Christ's death: "It breaks the power of cancelled sin." This is wonderful news for the believer.

29

Not only is our sin cancelled through faith in Christ, meaning that we're free from its penalty, but there's also the fact that its power over us is broken, meaning we're freed from a sin-dominated life. We no longer need to let sin reign - indeed we're told not to. Sin is no longer our master or boss. But as we've said, although it's dethroned it's not destroyed, so we needn't think that we won't sin - it's just that we don't have to, we're not obliged to.

It was some time after I'd been baptized by immersion that I understood Romans chapter 6 to teach that my baptism was not so much announcing to those who witnessed it that "Jesus had died for me" but more that "I'd died with Jesus," and that death had released me from being a slave to sin, had broken the power of cancelled sin in my life and so made possible for me to walk in newness of life as a servant of God instead. What we've learned from those stones at the Jordan can really make a powerful difference in your life and mine!

7

Reaching First Base

A t this point we remain encamped with the ark at Gilgal on the farther side of the Jordan river. The people have just crossed that river under Joshua's leadership. Gilgal was their first base in the land of promise and it became a sort of bridgehead for their early military offensives. We're keeping pace with the ark of the covenant, going with it on its historic Bible journey from Mount Sinai to Mount Sion, or Jerusalem. As we've moved along with it so far, we've already pointed out Old Testament illustrations of New Testament teaching for us as Christians today. But, as we'll see today, I hope, there are also lessons to be learnt from the places where it was stationed for a while. Gilgal was one of those places, the first in the land of Canaan, or the promised land to the Israelites.

While the ark remained stationed with the people at Gilgal, some very important things took place there - things from which we can draw spiritual lessons today. Early in Joshua 5 Joshua was told to circumcise the people for the second time. For the second time? Wait a minute - what does that mean? The Bible gives us the explanation that all the generation who'd been circumcised in Egypt had died in the wilderness; and all those born in the desert, the wilderness generation, had never been circumcised in the wilderness. Now, at their first base in the land, it was time for this to be rectified. When Joshua had finished using the flint knives, the LORD said to him, "This day I have rolled away the reproach of Egypt from you" (Joshua 5:9). It was as though the wilderness years of defeat were now to be put behind them for good.

What can we learn from this? Well, one thing's for sure: a life of defeat is always going to be a reproach to God. God's ideal with circumcision was that it shouldn't have remained an outward thing. Circumcision then was literally in the flesh, but there should have been something inward corresponding to it – Romans 2:29 calls it "a circumcision of the heart." What's more, Paul, in writing to the Colossians in chapter 2 and verse 11, applies the teaching of circumcision to believers today in this sense, saying that in Christ we "were also circumcised with the circumcision made without hands by putting off the body ... of the flesh, by the circumcision of Christ." This is something which is spiritual and entire in the case of every believer.

It was at salvation in our experience that the Lord, in a spiritual surgical act, dealt with the uncircumcision of our flesh – our old sin nature – which was so unprofitable to him. After we're saved, our responsibility is to live up to this. That's why the Bible speaks of us still having to put off the flesh, that is, our old sin nature. We're to see ourselves as God sees us now in Christ. We're to become in practical terms what we already are by his grace. This we must do, for remember, the lesson of Gilgal is that a life of defeat is a reproach to God. Either we'll be victimized by the flesh or conquered by the Spirit of God. Like the Israelites then, let's submit to the knife without fear - for it's in the hand of our Lover, the Lord whose Word, Hebrews 4:12 tells us, is sharper than any two-edged sword.

It's a personal question that comes to our hearts from this: 'Can we look back to a time or place in our Christian experience when we definitely renounced "the lusts of the flesh" - as the Bible puts it - and all the reproach associated with them?' Romans chapter eight, the early verses of the chapter, make it very clear to us that before we came to know Jesus Christ as our personal Saviour we were "in the flesh" (v.8); whereas now as believers we can be described as "in the Spirit" (v.9). However, though we are "in the Spirit" as believers, we could still live our lives "according to the flesh" (v.4). A life like that would be a life of defeat and reproach for a believer. God wants us to live "according to the Spirit" (v.4).

Gilgal, this first station of the ark of the covenant whose travels we're following, was also a place of remembrance as well as a place of renunciation. For after 3 days there, they kept the Passover. By keeping the Passover, they were remembering what the Lord had done for them in bringing them out of Egypt by the slaying of the lambs. For each household of Israel, the Passover lamb, was killed; but among the Egyptians who were not protected in this way, the firstborn son in each family died in the judgement of that tenth and final plague. It was God's will for the Israelites to remember this passover every year at the same time - to remember what he'd done for them to set them free.

This also has its counterpart today for the Lord wants us to remember what he did for us at the cross. As the apostle Paul says, Christ our passover was slain for us (1 Corinthians 5:7). The Lord has said in his Word to us: "Remember Me." And, knowing how short our memories are, he commands us in his Word to do this every week: to remember him in the emblems of the bread and the wine. It's a reminder, too, that we're working from victory. If Gilgal, as we've seen, was a place of renouncing, as well as a place of remembering; then it was also equally a place of removing. It was there God removed the manna from the children of Israel. After the Passover celebrations Joshua and the people began to eat the produce of the land. Up till then they'd still been eating the manna, which was the special bread supplied daily from heaven. It's always God's purpose to move us from the exceptional and extreme to the normal supplies of his grace. The supernatural deliveries of heavenly bread ended there at Gilgal. It was the same in the time of Jesus' life on earth – there was a demand for signs and wonders, but the normal Christian experience is to know by faith the supplies of his grace through the sometimes perplexing difficulties of life. We're strengthened by his grace as we derive our sustenance and power by faith from his risen life.

Before we take our leave of Gilgal, let's note another very significant thing that happened there – Joshua met the Lord! In those days when Moses was the leader and Joshua was Moses' assistant; Joshua, like the others, would only ever see the reflected glory of the Lord as it shone afterwards in the face of Moses after he'd been speaking with him. Now, it was Joshua's turn to be actually face to face with the Lord. We read that "a Man stood opposite him" – a man who revealed himself as the

Commander of the army of the LORD. There, so reminiscent of Moses' burning bush experience, Joshua was told to take off his sandals for the place was holy where he stood.

"Face to face shall I behold Him," the hymn says. And the apostle John comments: "When we see Him we shall be like Him." What a wonderful prospect! Ah, you say, but that's future, and so it is, for we wait his soon appearing to take us home. But I do believe that there in John's words we have the great secret of our lives - for it's in seeing him that we can become like him. 'When we see Him we shall be like Him', the apostle John says. That can be our spiritual experience now - seeing him as he revealed himself to the two on the way to Emmaus - that is, seeing him in all the Scriptures while their physical recognition of him was prevented.

John 14 tells us that if we love him he'll manifest himself to us. He'll manifest himself to us in our Bibles. "Beyond the sacred page I see Thee, Lord," the hymn says. But it demands holy living, of course, since Hebrews 12 speaks of the sanctification without which no one shall see the Lord. That's now! And to see him is to be like him! Surely we long to see him in our daily Quiet Times and to have the kind of daily briefing from our great Captain that Joshua received that day when he communed with him and said "What does my Lord say to His servant?"

8

Overcoming the World

H aving followed the ark of the covenant on its journey from Mount Sinai, we've seen how it played an important role in the crossing of the Jordan river and how its first base in the land was at Gilgal. We're now moving on with the ark to Jericho - to the first battle and the first victory in the land of promise, the land of Canaan.

Remember, before the battle the Lord had appeared to Joshua and told him how he would get the victory. First of all the Lord had said to Joshua, "See! I have given Jericho into your hand." Can you just imagine Joshua looking at Jericho and staring up at those famous walls while being asked to believe it was as good as captured already? Talk about a test of faith! But isn't it true to our experience of God? He doesn't remove the Jerichos from our lives. He doesn't remove the things that test our faith in him. Instead, he invites us to see things as he sees them, to see things with the eye of faith.

Then the Lord went on to spell out to Joshua the special winning strategy that would succeed in overcoming and capturing this proud city. It wouldn't be a case of storming it with battering rams and engines of war. Basically, they were simply to walk around the city in procession once every day for 6 days, and then 7 times on the 7th day. In this chapter, the 6th of the book of Joshua, we again have 10 mentions of the ark of the covenant. It's the ark of God that we're paying special attention to, so it's very relevant for us to notice that it's mentioned no less than ten times in Joshua chapter 6. Its presence in that procession around the walls of Jericho was absolutely vital to the success of the whole enterprise. And, once again, we read in verse 6 that it was the priests that Joshua commanded to take up the ark at Jericho.

Day after day, the armed men went round as the advance party, followed by 7 priests blowing trumpets, followed in turn by the ark with the rest of the people bringing up the rear guard. During all this time the people had been told to say nothing. On the 7th day the usual circuit around Jericho was repeated another 6 times, then Joshua gave the command "Shout, for the LORD has given you the city!" It was then that the wall fell down and the invaders were able to go straight in and conquer the now defenceless city.

I like to view this story as a kind of picture of what the Lord has done at Calvary through his cross for each one of us who believes on him. I'm suggesting that it has to be a picture of the Lord and his working because of the prominence of the ark in this incident. 1 John 3:8 tells us that one of the reasons that Jesus was manifested was in order to destroy the works of the Devil. You remember the Lord's silence before Pilate and his accusers.

Then, on the cross at the end of the 3 hours of supernatural darkness, he cried out with a loud shout "It is finished." Just as when Joshua's army shouted and the walls of Jericho came crashing down, I like to think of that loud cry of the Saviour on the cross causing, in effect, Satan's bulwarks to be broken down.

Now, as believers on the Lord Jesus, we're working from victory, and its ours "to cast down strongholds" as 2 Corinthians 10:4 puts it, as we depend on him. Let's just consider again these words of Paul in 2 Corinthians 10:3-5: "For though we walk in the flesh, we do not war according to the flesh. For the weapons of our warfare are not carnal but mighty in God for pulling down strongholds, casting down arguments and every high thing that exalts itself against the knowledge of God, bringing every thought into captivity to the obedience of Christ."

These strongholds may be habits or thoughts that are opposed and exalted against God. But I want you to see that the war is won, our foe has been defeated without us having to fight for that victory at all - it was all the Lord's doing just as it was at Jericho. We say again our enemy, the Devil, is a defeated enemy, we only have his "wiles" left to contend with (Ephesians 6:11). And the wily old Devil that he is, he trips us up so easily at times when we're off guard by drawing us away after worldly things – the lust of the flesh; the lust of the eyes; and the vainglory of life, or proud ambition - that's how John puts it in his first letter and chapter 2 verse 16.

It's all illustrated in the events that happened after the victory at Jericho in the book of Joshua. The Lord had forbidden the Israelites to take for themselves any of the plunder of Jericho.

It must have been so tempting to pick up some of the beautiful articles from the ransacked houses. One man did. This serves as an example of the lust of the flesh. That one man's disobedience was the main reason for defeat in the next battle. Another factor contributing to defeat in the next battle was pride. The next city was a small one and the people were in buoyant mood following their easy victory over Jericho, so they decided what they would do without consulting the Lord who had given the previous victory. You see, they had come to believe in themselves. Pride had entered in. Needless to say, they were defeated until they dealt with the man who had disobeyed in taking plunder and until they had humbled themselves before the Lord.

Soon afterwards they were tricked by some people, called Gibeonites, into signing a peace treaty. God had forbidden the Israelites to make any agreements with any of the peoples of the land of Canaan, peoples who were steeped in evil and idolatry. But these Gibeonites were crafty. Although they were nearby, they dressed up their ambassadors in old clothes and gave them stale bread to carry. They were trying to give the impression that these messengers had travelled a long way and so it would be safe for the Israelites to make a peace agreement with them because they weren't close neighbours. The Israelites fell for it. If only they'd consulted their God, but they didn't. They took the decision on their own, according to the sight of their eyes.

Whether it's the lust of the flesh: in other words instant gratification; or whether it's selfish ambition: being driven by the urge for self-advancement; or whether it's the lust of the eyes: being overimpressed with the appearance of things - we can just as easily be tripped up into becoming worldly.

Thankfully, Joshua, in falling down before the ark (Joshua 7:6), shows us the way of recovery. We humble ourselves before the Lord and claim the provision of 1 John 1:9: "If we confess our sins, He is faithful and just to forgive us our sins and to cleanse us from all unrighteousness."

9

Judging the Wrong

T he archaeologists were puzzled at first as they tried to identify the ancient structure whose remains they had discovered on the hillside. What could it be, lying there on the slopes of the Mount Ebal of biblical fame in the land of Israel? Then someone remembered Joshua chapter 8 and the mention of an altar that Joshua had built on Mount Ebal in order to carry out an instruction given through Moses some while before. And so it turned out that, very possibly, the remains of this altar had been discovered.

It was back in Deuteronomy chapter 27 that Moses had com- manded the people that when they did finally enter the land of promise over the Jordan, they were to build an altar to the LORD in Mount Ebal and write the words of the Law upon its stones. Not far away lay the city of Shechem which has a famous Bible history, dating from the time of the patriarchs. Its name means shoulder, or saddle: a place of burden-bearing. It's easy to see geographically why it should be called this, for nearby rise the mountains of Ebal on the one side and Gerizim on the other. Shechem and its surrounding countryside form a sort of natural saddle shape between the two hills on either side. This was the spot chosen for the rehearsal of the curses and blessings of the Law; curses if the people disobeyed it and blessings if they obeyed.

In the time of Joshua, this command was carried out (as we read in Joshua chapter 8) once they'd crossed the Jordan. Six tribes of Israel were set on the one mountain and six on the other, and so the curse was rehearsed in the hearing of the people, being set upon Mount Ebal; while the contrasting blessings were recited upon Mount Gerizim. Perhaps the natural acoustics of the special geography of the place made it an ideal place for all the people to hear in that outdoors auditorium. It must have been an impressive demonstration of the two ways that have been set before mankind ever since the beginning, ever since Adam and Eve's eldest sons went their separate ways.

Psalm 1 highlights the contrast between the two for, you re-member, it speaks of "the way of the righteous" and "the way of the wicked." There the righteous are likened to an immoveable tree planted by the riverside, while the wicked are likened to the chaff (the refuse of the wheat) which the wind blows away:

> "Blessed is the man who walks not in the counsel of the ungodly, nor stands in the path of sinners, nor sits in the seat of the scornful; but his delight is in the law of the LORD, and in His law he meditates day and night. He shall be like a tree planted by the rivers of water, that brings forth its fruit in its season, whose leaf also shall not wither; and whatever he does shall

prosper. The ungodly are not so, but are like the chaff which the wind drives away. Therefore the ungodly shall not stand in the judgment, nor sinners in the congregation of the righteous. For the LORD knows the way of the righteous, but the way of the ungodly shall perish" (Psalm 1:1-6).

Isn't it interesting that the Law and the altar were placed on the mount of the curse, upon Ebal? Doesn't this suggest to us how, according to Galatians chapter 3, the Lord Jesus redeemed us from the curse of the Law when on the hill of Calvary? He became a curse for us even as it was written long before: "cursed is everyone that hangs on a tree." But where does the ark of the covenant come into all this, you may be wondering? Well, Joshua 8:33-34 tells us that the priests stood there at that time with the ark; and the people were divided in two: one lot on one side of the ark and the other half on the other side of it before the respective mountains:

> "Then all Israel, with their elders and officers and judges, stood on either side of the ark before the priests, the Levites, who bore the ark of the covenant of the LORD, the stranger as well as he who was born among them. Half of them were in front of Mount Gerizim and half of them in front of Mount Ebal, as Moses the servant of the LORD had commanded before, that they should bless the people of Israel. And afterward he read all the words of the law, the blessings and the cursings, according to all that is written in the Book of the Law."

At this solemn moment, the people of Israel made their commitment in the presence of the ark - and that's the last we hear of it in the book of Joshua. Let's be sure to commit ourselves in the presence of the Lord to the pathway of blessing for us. As it was then, God's way of blessing for us, his will for us, is the way that's according to his Word, the Bible. There are things called "blessings" today but they're not in accordance with God's Word, so as Christians we need to be on our guard. Moving through our Bible chronologically, we next meet the ark in the book and time of the Judges: "Then all the children of Israel ... went up and came to [Bethel] ... They sat there before the LORD and fasted that day until evening; and they offered burnt offerings and peace offerings before the LORD. So the children of Israel inquired of the LORD (the ark of the covenant of God was there in those days)" (Judges 20:26-27).

In that whole book of Judges, that reference in chapter 20 and verse 27 is the only reference to it. Now that's quite remarkable - only one mention of the ark in those days, despite God's will that it should have been central to the collective spiritual life of his people. Remember those great chapters of miracles and victory in Joshua 3 and also chapter 6, where the ark is mentioned 10 times in each chapter - no wonder there was victory. And no wonder here in the times of the Judges, with little care or attention paid to the ark, that we find that these were dark days for God's people. Like the church at Laodicea that we read of in Revelation 3 where Christ himself was shut outside, the people here, too, were in a poor spiritual state.

We read in this solitary reference that the ark was to be found at Bethel. Perhaps it was only temporarily stationed there. For in Joshua 18:1 we learn that the tabernacle, so presumably the ark, was set up at Shiloh, and that's certainly where we find it again in the first book of Samuel in the days of Eli. In the days of the judges when that single mention is made of the ark, it's at a time of judging a terrible wrong among God's people. That's very important. Up till now, as we've traced the ark on its journey, we've seen God's associated power dramatically demonstrated against the enemies of his people. But now we see it in the context of judging wrong within the people of God. Always, in every age, if we're to know power against external opposition, we'll also by the same token have to be prepared to experience God's convicting power within. We readily recall, I'm sure, the strong tone in many of the letters to the 7 churches of God towards the end of New Testament times, as recorded in the early chapters of the book of the Revelation.

And what of the expulsion of the immoral brother out of the Church of God in Corinth? In 1 Corinthians 5:4 Paul writes to them about this matter, that as gathered in the Name of the Lord Jesus and by his power, they were to deliver such a one to Satan, in other words to excommunicate him. A church of God, after the New Testament pattern, must be one which exercises such powerful scriptural discipline within its ranks and does not tolerate anyone or anything that's out of line with the Bible's teaching. Does that describe your church?

10

Prisoner of War!

As mentioned, it appears that from the time of Joshua 18 onwards the ark of the covenant was stationed at Shiloh. Shiloh had been deliberately chosen by God as his first dwelling place in the land of promise. Jeremiah 7:12 says: "Shiloh, where I caused My name to dwell at the first."

It's there that we read of young Samuel growing up "before the LORD." We read of Samuel settling down to sleep before the light of the lampstand in the tabernacle went out. That's actually quite a telling statement of those days, for the lamps were supposed to burn through the night until the morning. But things had gradually begun to fall by the wayside and it seemed that the whole vision of God living among his people - as symbolized in the ark - had begun to grow dim with the passage of the years. It was flickering and going out, just like the lamps. Eli, the old priest, was letting standards slip in his own family circle. Yet in all the darkness of those times, there was one bright light on the horizon. His name was Samuel. God had provided him to bring again better days for the people of

God.

We read of him lying down to sleep in the temple of the LORD where the ark of God was. Samuel was living close by the ark! That's where he was when God spoke to him. If we too live close to Christ we won't fail to hear his voice. Now when the LORD revealed Himself to Samuel in Shiloh by the Word of the LORD, the message was a message of judgement. Because Eli hadn't judged his sons, God would not only judge them but also the people. How it all came about makes solemn reading. Their enemy, the Philistines, came to war against Israel. In the first round of engagement, Israel came off worst. They held a post-mortem, but never prayed about it. They designed their own strategy of deliverance. They fetched the ark of God from the tabernacle at Shiloh and brought it to the battlefield. There came a great buzz of expectancy through the Israelite camp, for now God was with them, or so they thought.

However, the unthinkable happened. The battle again went disastrously wrong, Eli's sons who were accompanying the ark as priests were killed and the sacred ark itself was captured by the pagan Philistines. Imagine it, God's holy ark taken as a Philistine prisoner-of-war! But worst of all was the fact that God's presence left Shiloh altogether. It's to this time that the words of Psalm 78 apply - verse 60 onwards says: "So that He [that's God] forsook the tabernacle of Shiloh, the tent which He placed among men; and delivered His strength into captivity [that's a reference to the ark] and His glory into the adversary's hand."

What had gone wrong? They had thought more of the ark

than of God himself. They looked to the sacred chest to bring them victory by its presence on the battlefield. They revered the external form of their religion but had lost real spiritual connection with God. Like those about whom Paul later wrote to Timothy: they held a form of godliness, but had denied the power of it (2 Timothy 3:5).

We find something similar in the story of Gehazi, the servant of Elisha, the man of God. When he laid the prophet's staff on the face of a dead child it had no effect. The raising of the child had to await the arrival of Elisha himself (2 Kings 4:29,31). Then in the next chapter, after Elisha has healed Naaman of his leprosy and refused to take a present from him, we find Gehazi sneaking out after Naaman to obtain some of the offered wealth for himself (2 Kings 5:26,30). The facts seem to fit Paul's description to Timothy of those who are "lovers of money ... having a form of godliness but denying its power" (2 Timothy 3:2,5). Gehazi embodies that kind of greedy, power-denying form - a mere external form of religion, without inner substance or reality.

In contrast there were believers in Rome, to whom Paul wrote in chapter 6 (v.17), who were obeying "from the heart that form of doctrine" to which they'd been delivered. It's our duty to ensure by God's help that the form of teaching we find in the New Testament isn't practised by us in such a way that it becomes a mere impotent form, an institutionalised form, a fossilized form. This is the kind of thing we were thinking about with Israel and the ark of God when they'd thought to take it into battle - when they looked to the sacred chest to bring them victory by its presence on the battlefield. They revered the external form of their religion but had lost real spiritual connection with God.

The lessons for us are obvious, aren't they? We must beware of slipping into a powerless, rigid formality or legalism which knows or experiences little of the power and presence of the risen Christ. That is a recipe for defeat wherever and whenever it happens. But God is certainly not powerless, although our experience of him may be. That was what the Philistines, in turn, were to discover. For wherever the ark went throughout their territory it brought plague and mayhem. When they put it in the house and temple of their god, Dagon, they found the idol smashed on the floor in front of it, for what communion has light with darkness? And Dagon, the fish-god, was definitely deep darkness for some think this was just another form of the old Babylonian mystery religion, so opposed to God and hated by God.

The ark wouldn't be allowed to remain there for long. It would have to be separated from these things. The temple of God has no fellowship with idols. This is a far-reaching principle, and one which the apostle Paul expressed to believers in the Church of God at Corinth as he wrote his second letter to them. He warns:

> "Do not be unequally yoked together with unbelievers. For what fellowship has righteousness with lawless-ness? And what communion has light with darkness? And what accord has Christ with Belial? Or what part has a believer with an unbeliever? And what agreement has the temple of God with idols? For you are the temple of the living God. As God has said: 'I will dwell in them and walk among them. I will be their God, and they shall be My people.' Therefore "Come

out from among them and be separate, says the Lord. Do not touch what is unclean, and I will receive you. I will be a Father to you, and you shall be My sons and daughters, says the Lord Almighty" (2 Corinthians 6:14-18).

These were believers living in New Testament times in the midst of a pagan culture. One of the big issues which surfaces in Paul's letters to them is about the business of eating food that'd been sacrificed to an idol. Food that'd been used as part of pagan religious rituals was often sold off cheaply it seems, making it an attractive buy. But was it right for a Christian to buy it and eat it? Basically Paul says they can, so long as they're clear in their minds about the evil of idolatry and have nothing to do with it, and so long as they give no offence to anyone else in eating the food. But it would be serious wrong for the believers to associate themselves with any of the pagan rituals and eat the same food in that way. Paul condemned eating "with consciousness of the idol" for eating the food "as a thing offered to an idol" was clearly wrong (1 Corinthians 8:7) - for the reason that sacrificing to idols involves fellowship with demons (1 Corinthians 10:20).

If a pagan neighbour had asked one of those Corinthian Christians to join him or her in an idol feast at a pagan temple - something which would've been quite a socially acceptable thing there in those times - that believer would be able to recall Paul's words from the Lord: "Do not be unequally yoked together with unbelievers ... what agreement has the temple of God with idols?" This is a far-reaching principle which the story of the ark of God in the Philistine temple has brought us on to. May God help us to live close to the Lord, to hear his voice, to catch the vision of his dwelling with us on the earth, and to separate from all that's contrary to his will for us.

11

Going by the Book

Have you ever doubted the sovereignty of God: the fact that he's in control? It's one thing to acknowledge it in our theology, but in practice we can sometimes deny it without realizing it. Sometimes we can act like the Philistines. Remember, when we last left the ark of the covenant it was in Philistine hands. When they placed it in the house of their god, Dagon, his image lay smashed before it in the morning. Wherever it visited throughout the five cities of the Philistine lords there was disaster and mayhem. At last, they had a committee meeting to decide what to do. The decision was to send the ark back to the Israelites on a cart or wagon. But to make sure that everything that had happened to them since its arrival wasn't just some strange string of coincidences, they agreed to stack the odds against the ark making it back.

They selected oxen that had never previously borne a yoke. In addition, the oxen had recently calved. Without guidance they were unlikely to head directly into Israelite territory. Natural instinct would be expected to draw them back to their calves.

However, as it turned out, the oxen pulled the wagon directly back to Israelite territory, to Bethshemesh in fact, confirming miraculously to the Philistines that the hand of God had been in all that had happened.

Do we sometimes say "If this happens ... and if such and such takes place ... then I'll know this is what God's asking me to do"? Do we, too, like the Philistines, attempt to overinsure ourselves against the possibility of mistaking the sovereign hand of God - perhaps it's because of a reluctance to accept it? When the inhabitants of Bethshemesh saw the ark returning, 1 Samuel 6 tells us they rejoiced to see it. Bethshemesh was a Levite city and so the ark of God would be especially meaningful to them. It reminds us of what's recorded of the Lord's disciples in John 20:20 when, in resurrection, it says that the disciples rejoiced and were glad to see the Lord. He'd come back from the dead. In fact, the ark's sojourn in enemy territory and its eventual return is in a sense a picture of the Lord's surrendering of himself to the hands of lawless men leading to his death and resurrection - the ark, as we've often said, representing Christ.

But the joy we experience at salvation and in early Christian life can become dulled - leading to the kind of state described in one of our hymns when it says, "Thy presence we have coldly sought" (PHSS 378). And so it was with the ark upon its return. After that initial joy at Bethshemesh, we read that during the days while Saul was king, it was simply left in Kiriath Jearim. In 1 Chronicles 13:3 we read that Israel didn't "seek unto" the ark during all the days of Saul. It just didn't seem to figure in Saul's plans or thinking.

What a contrast with the king who succeeded him! David, his successor, was a man after God's own heart - in other words he cared for the things God cared for and would do all God's will. When he came to the throne, after capturing Jerusalem, David made it a priority to fetch the ark up from the "fields of the woods" where Psalm 132 indicates it had lain throughout the reign of Saul. Just listen to David's attitude towards the ark:

> "Surely I will not go into the chamber of my house, or go up to the comfort of my bed; I will not give sleep to my eyes or slumber to my eyelids, until I find a place for the LORD, a dwelling place for the Mighty One of Jacob. Behold, we heard of it in Ephrathah; we found it in the fields of the woods Let us go into His tabernacle; let us worship at His footstool. Arise, O LORD, to Your resting place, you and the ark of Your strength. Let Your priests be clothed with righteousness, and let Your saints shout for joy" (Psalm 132:3-9).

David's first move in removing the ark to Jerusalem, however, was to prove to be a false one (as recorded in 2 Samuel 6:3-7). Perhaps influenced by what the Philistines had done, David set the ark on a wagon pulled by oxen. They hadn't gone far before the oxen stumbled and someone called Uzzah stuck out his hand to steady the ark. For doing what had long ago been forbidden to even the Levites - for touching the sacred chest that symbolized the presence of God - Uzzah was struck down dead by God. We don't know all that lay behind this. Uzzah was one of the family that had given shelter to the ark. Perhaps familiarity had bred contempt, and it come to be for him just that old box that stood in the corner of the house.

What we do know is that David caused the journey to be aborted. David might be surprised, confused, displeased and disappointed - but two clear commands of God's Word had been broken. As noted earlier, God had clearly said in the days of Moses that not even the Levites were to touch the ark - it was to be carried by staves upon their shoulders. Wagons could be used for transporting other tabernacle objects but not for the most holy ark, the ark of God. But the strange thing is that the Philistines appeared to have got away with this. Surely the lesson for us is obvious: that the people of God, those to whom he has revealed his will may not do as others do. Greater privilege brings greater responsibility.

Considering again how we earlier compared carrying the ark with our bearing testimony to Christ now, this should make us wary of enlisting new, worldly methods in proclaiming the gospel message and in taking forward the work of God. Secular techniques may work very well in modern business practice but aren't appropriate in bearing witness to Christ or serving him as Lord. The burden of the work of the Lord can't be rolled onto smooth self-sustaining organizations, but has to be shouldered by those who are devoted to the task, those who feel its weight of responsibility and its holiness. Reverence in the things of God calls for personal dedication.

We're rightly alarmed at any lack of evangelical progress, but let's take notice that there's a wrong way to support a tottering testimony. Steps that cut across the plain Word of God will be found to be false steps. The Philistines had previously carried the ark on a new cart, without consequence to them. Presumably, since they had no other instruction, they were genuinely trying to respect it by using something unpolluted. But David should have known better, even though his motives and desires were good. The lesson we can draw is that, in order to please God, right motives and desires are necessary but on their own they're not sufficient. Reverence for the things of God calls for obedience to God's revealed will which we find in our Bibles.

12

The Last Pilgrim in the Land!

W e've been considering David's ill-fated first attempt to bring the ark of the covenant up to Jerusalem. David records for us in Psalm 132 that he'd found it in "the field of the wood" - which seems to be a reference to Kiriath Jearim. David was genuinely troubled that God should now be the last pilgrim in the land! After all, he and all the people had their houses, but God's ark was still in a tent.

After seeing blessing in the house of Obededom where the ark had lain for three months since that first attempt, David again attempted to bring the ark to him at Jerusalem. This time he was successful because he was careful to do everything in accordance with God's Word. So the ark was brought into a tent at Jerusalem (1 Chronicles 16) while the other Tabernacle articles were still to be found at Gibeon. The Tabernacle itself seemed to move from Shiloh to Nob to Gibeon and then to Jerusalem.

Unlike Saul, David was giving God his rightful place. He wouldn't reign without him. It's worth pausing to consider our own experience, isn't it? What's our experience of reigning in life through Christ, as Romans 5:17 speaks of it? Or rather, does sin reign in our mortal bodies, despite the warning given against that in the next chapter, in Romans chapter 6? At the most practical level of our lives, what governs our decisions - is it God, or money, or some other thing? We can't reign in life without him. Let's be like David and give the Lord his rightful place in our lives.

While it was David who longed to build God a house, being disappointed that he still only had a tent, yet it was David's son, Solomon, whom God said would build his Temple at Jerusalem. After Solomon had completed the project, taking seven years to do it, 1 Kings 8:6 tells us that once again on this special occasion it was the priests that brought the ark into the Temple. But, before he died, David, although not allowed to build the house since he'd been a man of war, was nevertheless given the plan of how it was to be built and also shown the site God had chosen.

In a most miraculous way the site for the permanent house for the ark, the Temple for God to dwell in, was revealed by God to David as being the area of a threshing-floor belonging to a man called Ornan. Threshing-floors are an important study in the Bible: symbolizing the twin processes of separation and gathering. God has a lot to say to us in his Word about those two spiritual processes, both in our personal lives and in our collective service with others. In Matthew chapter 3, John the Baptist foretold of the coming Messiah who would thoroughly cleanse His threshing-floor and gather the wheat, the good grain, into his granary or barn.

The threshing-floor of Bible times was often simply an elevated flat rock where oxen were made to pull heavy wooden implements around over the newly harvested grain as it was strewn on the rocky surface. The result of this was a crude separation of the good grain from the useless "chaff." The separation process was fully effected through what was known as "winnowing." This was when the grain and chaff mixture was hoisted up into the air using a large kind of fork, sometimes called a "fan." The evening breeze then blew away the lighter chaff, leaving the heavier grain to fall down and be left behind on the threshing-floor ready to be gathered into the granary for use.

At a personal level, this relates to the work of God in our lives, separating good from evil. There's no chaff permitted in his granary. When God gathers, it's as much about quality as about quantity. But here in this context it has to do with the building of God's house. Is there an equivalent building today? Yes, there is according to 1 Peter 2:5: "You also as living stones are being built up to be a spiritual house." The New Testament teaches us how the principles of separation and gathering are basic to the thought of God's house.

Whenever God's pattern for how he is to be served was threatened by other religions, by different teachings or by sectarian divisions, in every case God's will was reinforced - Christians must remain separate from Judaizers, from false teachers, from those who chose rather their own way and caused divisions. The full gospel isn't purely a matter of sowing and reaping; it's a matter of sowing, reaping, threshing and separating. These are matters we need to give attention to. This is a separation from all that isn't in harmony with God's will revealed in Scripture -

a separation from all that's worldly, from unbiblical practices – accompanied by a gathering of ourselves to the Name of the Lord Jesus. This is the Bible picture of churches of God - it's one of separated disciples, gathered out from the world and gathered together on the basis of God's pattern for our collective service - all the churches with one teaching, each individual person ministering their gift, and the whole thing - as a house for God - under a fellowship of lay elders.

The main steps the early Christians went through in putting God's will into effect are summarized in Acts 2:41,42: "Then those who gladly received his word were baptized; and that day about 3000 souls were added to them. And they continued steadfastly in the apostles' doctrine and fellowship, in the breaking of bread, and in prayers." If you're a Christian but feel, like the ark of God in David's day, that you've not found your home yet within God's house today, do feel free to write to the author and ask for further explanation of these important matters, for we're coming now to the end of our journey in which we've been travelling along with the ark of God. We trust and pray that its lessons by the help of the Spirit of God will serve to enrich our spiritual walk, witness and warfare.

MORE BOOKS FROM BRIAN JOHNSTON

Our God Reigns! The Awesome Sovereignty of God

"We are still masters of our fate. We still are captains of our souls," said Winston Churchill in World War 2, paraphrasing a fragment of a famous poem also admired by Nelson Mandela. Perhaps it's become a cultural meme, but is it in step with the Bible's theme? Can we control our own destiny, or is it all down to chance? Who, or what, is in charge of history?

To be credible, any worldview must answer four questions - about our origins, our morality, our (life's) meaning, and our destiny. When the author's daily Bible readings took him to Isaiah 37-47, he found the Biblical worldview does just that in an impressive declaration and demonstration of the sovereignty of God. That's what led to the writing of this book, which along the way seeks to answer some important questions that have puzzled people for centuries:

- What does the Bible categorically say about human origins?
- Does God change his mind?
- Why did God order the killing of peoples in the Old Testa-

ment?
- Has Israel been left out of God's purposes?
- Why bother praying?
- Was Jesus' crucifixion simply a terrible accident?
- Does God decide who is saved and who isn't?
- What are God's purposes in the end times?
- Does man have free wills?
- Do the sign gifts operate today in God's purposes?

Sowing in Hard Soil: Tools and Encouragement for Preaching the Gospel

On a few occasions in the New Testament, the Apostle Paul urges his readers not to lose heart. In particular, he appeals that they don't lose heart in evangelism. This appeal can be found – twice in fact - in 2 Corinthians 4. If we're in the western world today, it's not hard to appreciate why he had this concern. Paul encountered in certain places the same stony indifference we can come up against, ranging even to outright hostility at times. We can all too readily identify the same features in society around us that the Apostle Paul diagnoses in the Greco-Roman world of the first century AD (Romans 1). Drawing from Paul's writings, Bible teacher and broadcaster Brian Johnston provides a number of tools and also some encouragement in preaching the gospel in modern society.

Does Anyone Know Why We're Here? Answers from Ecclesiastes

Ravi Zacharias, a Christian apologist, was once speaking to a large college crowd when he was suddenly interrupted. A student stood up and yelled, "Everything is meaningless!" Zacharias responded, "You don't believe that." The student yelled back, "Yes, I do!" "No, you don't." "I most certainly do. Who are you to tell me I don't?" "Then repeat your statement for me." "Everything is meaningless!" Ravi then said, "If your statement is meaningful, then everything is not meaningless. On the other hand, if everything is meaningless, then what you have just said is meaningless too. So, in effect, you have said nothing. You can sit down."

The consideration of whether it could be true that everything is meaningless is not a consideration we expect to find arising from within a biblical worldview, where God is accepted as existing and giving meaning and purpose to human existence. But the curious thing – at least at first sight – is that one entire book in the Bible is devoted to exploring whether or not everything is meaningless. Why should this be the case? Bible teacher and broadcaster Brian Johnston gives the answer.

Going the Distance: How to Avoid a Spiritual Knock-out

The Christian life is a marathon, not a sprint. It's a contest with many rounds, not just one. Comparing Christians to athletes, and personalizing it, the Apostle Paul says: "... I run in such a way, as not without aim; I box in such a way, as not beating the air; but I discipline my body and make it my slave, so that, after I have preached to others, I myself will not be disqualified" (1 Corinthians 9:26-27). The picture of a boxer is especially apt, as experience teaches us that we don't need to go very far in the Christian life before we start taking 'blows' or 'hits.'

In another place, Paul talks about being "struck down" (2 Corinthians 4:9). He goes on to make it clear that he was down, but not out. But, sadly, for many today the 'knock-out' rate is high. What are those 'hooks' that leave many sprawling on the canvas? They are the same ones that godly people have been experiencing since Bible times. This book by Bible teacher and broadcaster Brian Johnston attempts to bring together some of the notable 'sucker punches' that often get thrown at Christians - discouragement, guilt, failure, anxiety, distraction, lust, anger, pride, doubts, greed, divisions and disappointments. It aims to help us to draw on the resource of the Bible's guidance to enable us to keep our guard up.

ABOUT THE AUTHOR

Born and educated in Scotland, Brian worked as a government scientist until God called him into full-time Christian ministry on behalf of the Churches of God (www.churchesofgod.info). His voice has been heard on Search For Truth radio broadcasts for over 30 years (visit www.searchfortruth.podbean.com) during which time he has been an itinerant Bible teacher throughout the UK. His evangelical and missionary work outside the UK is primarily in Belgium, The Philippines and South East Central Africa. He is married to Rosemary, with a son and daughter.

`

ABOUT THE PUBLISHER

Hayes Press (www.hayespress.org) is a registered charity in the United Kingdom, whose primary mission is to disseminate the Word of God, mainly through literature. It is one of the largest distributors of gospel tracts and leaflets in the United Kingdom, with over 100 titles and many thousands dispatched annually. In addition to paperbacks and eBooks, Hayes Press also publishes Golden Bells, a popular daily Bible reading calendar in wall or desk formats.

If you would like to contact Hayes Press, there are a number of ways you can do so:

By mail: c/o The Barn, Flaxlands, Royal Wootton Bassett, Wiltshire, UK SN4 8DY

By phone: 01793 850598

By eMail: info@hayespress.org

via Facebook: www.facebook.com/hayespress.org

www.ingramcontent.com/pod-product-compliance
Lightning Source LLC
Chambersburg PA
CBHW071848020426
42331CB00007B/1906